How
I Overcame
Abuse

My Struggle to Become Whole
After Molestation and Rape

Patricia Edwards-Burton

ISBN 978-1-0980-5829-6 (paperback)
ISBN 978-1-0980-5830-2 (digital)

Christian Faith Publishing, Inc.
832 Park Avenue
Meadville, PA 16335
www.christianfaithpublishing.com

Printed in the United States of America

ACKNOWLEDGMENTS

Thanks to my mom who has been a strong support in my life and my daughters for being good children and for not giving me too many gray hairs; my dear husband who continues to stand by my side and is a strong sense of support; and my younger sister as a good source of encouragement.

CONTENTS

Introduction

I am sharing my experience as a source of encouragement to help someone reach into one's self as I have and unlocked the shame and discouragement of hidden secrets of molestation and rape so that healing can be promoted. Your experience can be shared to help others who have endured similar trauma in life, and this book is to let you know that even through struggles and life's perplexities, we can overcome hardship and challenges by trusting in God and having faith through a life of prayer. Life's circumstances may arise, but we do not have to be defeated or succumb to life's pressures. We can be overcomers and go on to have an enjoyable life, even when faced with difficulties.

1
WHO IS NOBLE PATRICIA?

I was born in Birmingham, England, to West Indian parents in a family of eight girls and three boys. I was the sixth child. While my mom resided in St. Ann, Jamaica, my oldest sister, died. She became ill and lost her life. My mom then migrated to England where a second daughter died in a fire, so I lost two older siblings prior to my birth.

It makes me wonder today, if they had been alive, how my life would be different. Maybe I would have been more protected. Maybe I would have had a happier childhood. I was a quiet child, yet happy-go-lucky; not many things bothered me.

My two older brothers joined us, migrating from St. Ann, Jamaica. My older brother was my favorite because he was cool and made time for me as the sixth child in a large family. My sisters and I would play together. We were a poor family, and there were quite a few mouths to feed, so we did not have toys. We would cut dolls out of pillow cases, sew them together, and stuff them; then we would draw a face, and that was our toy. We would sit around the fireside and play games and talk. We read a lot of books; my parents encouraged us to read.

My dad married my mom, and my mom's brother married my dad's sister; it was a unique bond. Together, my uncle and my aunt had two children, a boy and a girl.

> O Lord thou hast searched me, and known me.
> Thou knowest my down sitting and mine upris-
> ing, thou understandest my thought afar off.

9

Thou compasseth my path and my lying down, and art aquainted with all my ways. For there is not a word in my tongue, but lo, O Lord thou knowest it altogether. (Psalms 139:1–3)

My substance was not hid from thee, when I was made in secret, and curiously wrought in the lowest parts of the earth. Thine eyes did see my substance, yet being unperfect; and in thy book all my members were written, which in continuance were fashioned, when as yet there was none of them. (Psalms 139: 15–16)

This scripture spoke to me because it reminded me that I was loved and served a God who cares in spite of the evil we may encounter in the world today. The Lord blessed us to be together as a family. We were handpicked by God. He knows all about us, our high points and our low points. He loves us with an everlasting love, and no matter what, God cares.

2

FACING CHANGES

Growing up in the city of Birmingham in England was where I began to experience life in this world of possibilities and embarked on a life of prayer. We were brought up as a family in the Apostolic Church where we attended church on a regular basis. We were taught Christian values and baptism in Jesus's name, being filled with the Holy Spirit, and living a holy life. We attended Sunday school where we were taught the scriptures and Bible verses. We had Sunday school programs in which we sang and recited poems. We also attended Sunday school excursions to the beach and various different places.

At the tender age of approximately seven, I was molested by a family member. This act totally changed my life having been robbed of my innocence at such a young age. As a result, I stopped applying myself in school and kept quiet because I did not know who to share this with. This memory caused me to continue on in life as an introverted child.

While attending a Sunday service, I felt a call to get baptized in Jesus's name at the church we were attending. I got baptized at the age of thirteen. Being an observant child, I watched the bishop as he ushered prayer in the sanctuary and noted that he prayed for long periods at a time, sometimes in tears.

Therefore, I mimicked his practice and began a life of prayer. Praying brought about peace. I had to believe in order to pray because God was not tangible. I would sing from the hymnal songs of God's love and be brought to tears at a young age. Jesus became a rock in which I could lean on and pour out in times of uncertainty. Being brought up in the Apostolic Church, this was what I knew to do.

My dad migrated to the United States in search of a better life. At the age of sixteen, I joined him along with my older sister, leaving behind my mother along with my four sisters and my youngest brother. My parents agreed to send my older sister and I because we were older.

Life with my dad was calm. He was a strict father. We could not do as we pleased. We had to follow the rules of the house. My dad did not approve of us wearing pants or jewelry. We had to wear skirts and dresses. Dad kept to himself outside of making sure we were fed and a roof was over our heads. He took a live-in job as a home health aide to pay the mortgage and the bills. He was not a talkative person, but we knew he was there for us.

Life in America was different, and it was an adjustment. The food was different, and I got teased at school because my accent was different. We attended the local high school. I began in the eleventh grade. My application toward school was poor. My older sister, in my mother's absence, became the mother figure. She got a job after graduating high school and bought my clothes and did some of the cooking while I helped and did the housekeeping.

My dad and mom purchased a home. We moved in shortly after and picked out our bedrooms. This was exciting—our first home in the United States!

We attended the Apostolic Church of Jesus Christ in the area where my father was an active member. At church, I became vice president of the youth department. With this newfound position, we would put together puzzles and assignments for the youth. I spent much time in prayer for direction and guidance from the Lord to assist in leading the youth. My past did not surface. I stuck to the task at hand.

After graduating high school, I went on to attend Sheridan Vocational School where I graduated as a practical nurse. My mom was in England for my high school graduation and my graduation as a practical nurse. When I was a little girl, I wanted to become a nurse. I loved taking care of my dolls.

Despite the tragedy that happened in my childhood, I still became a nurse. I took my career seriously and was completely dedicated to helping others who needed care. I give God thanks I never gave up on my dream. Furthermore, I was able to fulfil what I believe was part of my destiny and God-given calling. I faced some painful moments, yet God allowed me to keep parts of myself that define who I am.

I missed my mom dearly. She was the glue that held our family together. Mom was a caring and loving person. She also had a positive spin on issues. My mom then joined us in the United States after a few years, leaving my sisters and brother with my aunt.

While at home, feeling depressed and wondering what to do with my life with the shadow of molestation hanging over me, I attempted to commit suicide by swallowing a bottle of aspirin. Strangely enough, I vomited up the tablets without even knowing God had a mark on my life.

God kept me here for a purpose. It was not time for me to leave this world yet. My mom was not privy to what had taken place. During this tumultuous time, I did not want to live. I felt there was no reason to go on with the trauma of molestation making me feel less than. My thoughts appeared stunted because this took place at a young age, which made it difficult to trust and make friends. I could not seem to get beyond this pain alone because I did not know how to reach out and share. I continued to attend church and continued in prayer for some guidance and direction from God and how to be happy in life.

3

THE HORROR OF A SECRET ACT

The molestation was not a touch. It was a selfish act from a perpetrator who was thinking solely of himself. The memory is vague, but the damage was done. It altered my childhood. I had to find ways to cope with this new normal. I had been changed. It was reeling in my mind how to think and act, but I had no answers. I did not understand what happened completely, but I knew I had been violated for no reason of my own. I was a happy-go-lucky kid who was friendly. I became quiet and kept to myself. I did not know how to share or who to share this act with. I put it out of my mind, and it became a memory.

The joy of being a little girl was gone. It seemed as if I was a shell of a person. Even though I was not able to understand the magnitude of what had taken place, the damage was done. When I was bullied at school, I got into a fight with a kid who would not leave me alone. I believe I took out some of my anger on him because he was disheveled. I was sent to the office and punished with a slap of a ruler in my hand.

The molestation made it difficult to trust anyone with my children. Everyone who came into our path I analyzed to see if they could be trusted. I was suspicious of everyone. I watched how people would interact with my children to determine how they would be treated. This took its toll because after a while, it became a burden to constantly check and second-guess to make sure they were safe.

My older daughter began to pull away because she could not handle me being so protective. I had to find more subtle ways of being protective. I could not stop because I knew the reason for the protectiveness. Eventually, I took my daughter out to her favorite restaurant and shared with her the rape and advised her to be cautious. Surprisingly, she said to me, "You should have told me earlier because I would be a stronger person." It was at a later date I shared the molestation.

4

OVERCOMING GRACE

While working at the hospital at the age of twenty-two, I noted a cloud of sadness over me, so I went to a doctor who prescribed Wellbutrin, an antidepressant to help with the sadness. However, soon after, while working at the hospital on the night shift and not resting enough, working and going to church between shifts, I began feeling like there was no reason to live. I was not happy, I felt inadequate and insecure within myself, and it was as if I blended in with the walls. It was difficult trying to be happy. I had no interest in sports or going to the mall to shop. I just wanted to be alone. This led to a nervous breakdown. The nervous breakdown made me more withdrawn into myself. I did not have many friends and was not a person with the gift of the gab.

After having a nervous breakdown, I was hospitalized for depression. I found myself sitting at a table, having a snack, when my mom and older sister came to visit me at the hospital. It was then for the first time that I opened up about being violated by a family member. The silence was gripping. Neither my mom nor my sister spoke for a short time. I felt lost and in a place of despair, not knowing what to do or how to move forward.

My parents and my sisters stood by me at this time. They were concerned and supportive. My mom said, "I tried everything to prevent this from happening."

My older sister never said a word.

When my condition improved, I was discharged from the hospital with a prescription for medication to help with depression and insomnia. While recuperating at home, I was invited to a friend's house to recuperate from the nervous breakdown. I went and was raped by one of her acquaintances and thereby gave birth to a baby girl. A month later, my daughter needed to have her checkup, so I asked her father for a ride to the doctor. After she was seen, he took me to his place. He said to me I had to do this, and he dragged me to the back room. I was kicking and fighting him off. He overpowered me and then raped me again. Remarkably, my daughter slept through it.

This was the last thing I had in mind after giving birth. Later, I found out he wanted another baby. That is when I embarked on the struggle of being a single mother. It was approximately a year later when I was in the right frame of mind and thought I should have called the authorities. I became paranoid and did not trust anyone. Everywhere I would go in society, I'd look over my shoulder, not knowing who would be lurking, trying to do me harm.

I got a job as a weight-loss counselor and had to open the place of business to start my shift. It was nerve-racking because if it was a male client to be seen that day, I would be afraid and nervous because of my past experience. I did not know how to communicate my fears, so I kept it to myself. Around this time, I'd been placed on benefits due to depression, and funds were limited. The single-parent struggle was real, yet I kept praying while living from paycheck to paycheck and looking for things to improve. I eventually had to sue the father for child support to help raise my child. He was not pleased and began to stalk me to drop the suit. I continued with the process for child support until it was final.

During this time, we were on Section 8, being assisted by the government to pay rent. The struggle was real. I had to cope with depression, and being a single mother, yet through this time, my faith kept me going. Even when I could not see how we were going to make ends meet, I kept crying out to God and trusting him to see us through. I raised my daughter with the help of my family members. My sisters were a great help with babysitting and purchasing some of her clothes.

My dad became a father figure to my daughter, even though he was Grandpa. My daughter would ask for her father. I did not know what to tell her, but I knew it was not healthy for him to be in our lives. I became a protective mother, always checking and double-checking to make sure all was well.

> The Lord is my Shepherd I shall not want. He maketh me to lie down in green pastures; he leadeth me beside still waters. He restoreth my soul; he leadeth me in the paths of righteousness for his name sake. Yea though I walk through the valley of the shadow of death, I will fear no evil; for thou art with me; thy rod and thy staff they comfort me. (Psalms 23:1–4)

This scripture was a blessing because no matter how difficult it was to make ends meet, there was always bread on the table.

Due to my disability, I could not work as a licensed practical nurse, so I took a job at the dollar store to help with our financial situation. This was a humbling experience, and I took a drastic pay cut. Strangely, the money that came in was enough to pay the day care, and after that was paid, there were a few dollars left over.

One Sunday, I went to church with my younger sister, and she was wearing a beautiful lilac-colored jacket, and I said in my thoughts, *That's a nice jacket.*

When I got home, the phone rang. My sister said to me, "This jacket is too big for me. Do you want it?"

I was overjoyed because we were struggling to make ends meet. I wore the jacket with pride.

> But my God shall supply all your needs according to his riches in glory by Christ Jesus. Now unto God and our Father be glory forever and ever. Amen. Whatever I needed no matter what it was I would put it before the Lord. (Philippians 4:19–20)

> Trust in the Lord all thine heart; and lean not unto thine own understanding. In all thy ways acknowledge him, and he shall direct thy path. The word of God has been a strong support in my life it's been my rock and strength. (Proverbs 3:5–6)

The Word is a guide and a great source of encouragement. No matter which challenge I faced, I was able to persevere by way of the Word or a song or a message from the preaching of the Word by attending church services over the years. Sustenance came from the Word.

> Finally, my brethren, be strong in the Lord, and in the power of his might. Put on the whole armor of God, that ye may be able to stand against the wiles of the devil. (Ephesians 6:10–11)

> Above all, taking the shield of faith, wherewith ye shall be able to quench all the fiery darts of the wicked. (Ephesians 6:16)

The Word of God would give me strength and uplift my spirit so I was able to move forward step-by-step. These scripture verses remind me that we will be tried and tested, but God will see us through.

5
PERSEVERANCE

While living on Section 8 as a single parent, I was at work, and my daughter was at day care. Our apartment was broken into and vandalized. The apartment was ransacked, and a television was stolen. Once again, I sought the Lord, not quite understanding why these events were unfolding. I needed to be somewhere safe, so I prayed for an apartment on the second floor.

A young lady who owned a condo and was having difficulty paying the mortgage rented us the condo. It was an answer to prayer. The place was cozy and located on the second floor. I was overjoyed, and my faith grew in God. Once again, my prayer was answered.

Seven years later, we moved in with my parents due to loneliness and an inability to cope on my own as a single mom. My daughter's father showed up and demanded to be a part of her life. I was floored! What was God going to do now? I did not trust him with the child. He was boasting how he was going to get a lawyer and sue me for visitation.

I went to see a lawyer of my own, one that was recommended by my pastor. The lawyer took my case. I used the money that was in my possession to pay the lawyer. This was not easy because money was tight, but I needed to have a defense. I could not lose this case. I asked my pastor to pray. He said, "The enemy does not triumph over God's people."

> Thou art my battle axe and weapons of war: for
> with thee will I break in pieces the nations, and with
> thee will I destroy kingdoms. (Jeremiah 51:20)

My younger sister called later that evening and said at church today, the minister was preaching about David and Goliath, how Goliath boasted and disrespected the children of Israel.

David was anointed and chosen by God for a purpose. He had proven in time past that God was a deliverer. He was not fearful. Goliath had no respect for God or the people of God. David was selected to let Goliath know that there was none greater than God.

When faced with adversities, we do not have to run away in fear. We can seek and trust God to deliver and bring about the victory. David believed because the Lord had delivered him from out of the paw of the lion and the paw of the bear that God would deliver him from this uncircumcised Philistine. I felt encouraged.

When the case was presented to the judge, she dismissed the case. I cried many tears. It was a relief. Once again, God had answered my prayers.

God is our refuge and strength, a very present help in trouble. (Psalms 46:1)

This scripture spoke to me because if I had lost the case, only God knows what the outcome would be, and the Lord God truly came through for me. I will forever be grateful.

6

MOVING FORWARD

While attending church, I decided I needed a husband, and my daughter needed a father. My interest in a certain individual piqued. It was rumored that I had compulsive disorder after being in counselling at the church. The rumor was false. I was a person who washed my hands frequently. Now looking back, I think I was trying to rid myself of the shame from the molestation and rape I had experienced.

One year, I was doing some charity work and had to deliver some goodies to a friend for the needy children. The day I was planning to go was Friday. However, because I had gathered so many items, I decided to deliver them a day earlier without any prior notice.

While I was there, my friend received a phone call from one of her friends. After a short while talking, she handed me the phone and said, "Talk to my friend until I come."

I took the phone and said hello. To my surprise, the person said, "Can I have your phone number please?"

I said, "You don't know me, why do you want my number?"

He said, "I like your accent and would like to hear it again."

When my friend returned, I told her what happened, and she was surprised, then said, "You can give it to him, he's a nice person."

So I did.

The next day, he called, checking out the number, and we had a long conversation, and from then, we talked almost every day.

He then invited me to England for my birthday, which was in May. I flew to England and met some of his family and had a great time. We hit it off right away. He was kind and easy to talk to. We dated for some time while I sought the Lord in prayer furthermore. I asked the pastor's wife to pray with me.

My husband and I corresponded back and forth. He then proposed one Sunday evening. I was delighted. He seemed like such a good man. I noted how caring and focused my husband was on planning the details of the wedding in London. It was an answer to prayer.

Holy matrimony took place in London, England, November 2003, and I returned to the United States while my husband continued to reside in London. It was a long-distance relationship. However, after two years, my husband joined me in the United States.

7
PERSISTENCE AGAINST ODDS

At this time, I was forty years old, and my biological clock was ticking, so we tried to have a baby. It was quite an experience because I got pregnant each year, and approximately after six weeks, I would lose the baby. This happened for three consecutive years. I was then sent to a specialist who diagnosed me with a condition called Antiphospholipid Syndrome, which means the baby is unable to thrive due to blood clots. Losing the babies was distressing because I was ready to have another child.

I went to Sunday evening service, and a young man was exhorting on the story of Hannah and Peninnah, how Hannah had no children for Elkanah. I felt impressed in my spirit that I was going to have another child.

After the third miscarriage, which was approximately in April, my husband and I came home from the hospital. I heard him praying about being a father, and I began to ponder if I had made the right decision by marrying because my husband had no children of his own.

I made an appointment to have my tubes flushed, only to find out the right one was blocked. The technician said to me, "Go home and baby dance."

It was approximately the month of June. I was pregnant and had to take injections every day for nine months for the Antiphospholipid Syndrome. Being pregnant was a joy and an answer to prayer. My dream of having another child was becoming a reality. It made me happy because I wanted to have another, even though I had lost three.

At this time, I was forty-three, experiencing a high-risk pregnancy from natural conception. I was ready for the challenge, or should I say the blessing. While pregnant for my husband, I was not worried about the pregnancy because it had been impressed on my spirit that I was going to have another child.

> For the Lord is good; his mercy is everlasting; and his truth endures to all generations. (Psalm 100:5)

As my younger daughter grew, my older daughter joined the United States Navy in pursuit of a career. This she continues to enjoy and is doing well. However, because she is away from home, I continue in prayer, trusting God to keep her safe and to bless her endeavors. Now that she is older, she reached out to her father, and they communicate from time to time.

8

DETERMINATION

Recently, I had a relapse because one of the medications I was on was no longer available. While the doctor tried me on several different medications to see what would work, I relapsed. It took its toll on the family yet once again. Even though I was not well, I kept praying and reaching out for God's help to get me through this time in my life.

> Be merciful unto me O Lord; for I cry unto thee daily. Rejoice the soul of thy servant: for unto thee, O Lord, do I lift up my soul. (Psalm 86:3–4)

This scripture was a comfort because I could continue to reach out to God and believe for change in my situation. Along with a supportive husband and family, I noted this time, I felt a sense of being delivered from everyday struggles. I had a sense of being able to reach out and trust again with a more positive outlook.

One day at home, all of a sudden, out of the blue, tears came to my eyes with tears streaming down. I thought about my dad whom I had not seen in several months due to my relapse. Later that day, I got a call from my younger sister who said, "Come to Mom's house right away." She would not disclose the reason for the haste.

Suspecting something was out of place, I pulled my younger daughter out of school, and we proceeded to Mom's. While in commute, my husband told me my dad had passed away that morning. The tears rolled down my face, but this time with an assurance, knowing Dad was in a better place.

It seemed to me thereafter that even though we were brought up in church and told about heaven for so many years, heaven seemed more real. Moreover, heaven appeared to be more attainable, even though I had heard of heaven for so many years.

My dad was in a better place and left behind a legacy for us to follow. Over the years, I was able to forgive those who wronged me, and I no longer feel like a victim but a survivor. Throughout the years, I'm consoled by prayer, reading the scriptures, and attending church. One of my favorite scriptures is Isaiah 54:17, "No weapon formed against thee shall prosper, and every tongue that shall rise against thee in judgement thou shalt condemn."

> My tears have been my meat day and night while they continually say, "Where is thy God?" (Psalms 42:3)

9

My Faith and How It Shaped Me

My faith shaped me because it taught me how to lean on a greater power, and not knowing how to share my experience, I was able to take it to the Lord in prayer. Along the way, I was encouraged by songs like "Learning to lean on Jesus, finding more power than I ever dream, I'm learning to lean on Jesus…"

> Thou wilt keep him in perfect peace, whose mind is stayed on thee: because he trusteth, in thee. Trust ye in the Lord forever: for in the Lord Jehovah is everlasting strength. (Isaiah 26:3–4)

I have learned and I'm still learning to trust in Jesus. I have found him to be a faithful God. One songwriter penned in a song "When nothing else could help, it was God's love that lifted me."

I would attend church and be encouraged by the presence of the saints—a smile, a hug, or a word of encouragement. I spent a lot of time in personal prayer, reaching out to God in search of how to get beyond abuse. I would pray about confidence and how to walk in the light. Christ is in the light.

> This then is the message which we have heard of him and declare unto you, that God is light and in him is no darkness at all. (1 John 1:5–7)

I would lean on God to provide everyday necessities—food, clothing, self-worth.

> But my God shall supply all your need according to his riches in glory by Christ Jesus. (Philippians 4:19)

10

The Damage Was Real
Suffering in Silence

The way I lost my virginity without consent affected me deeply because it was something. I could never give away willingly. I was brought up in the Apostolic Church, and we were taught to abstain until marriage. Being damaged at such a young age due to molestation and then rape made me feel unwanted. I was, as it were, damaged goods. I felt robbed because my virginity was taken. I wanted to share it with someone I loved. It took counselling to bring me to a place where I felt I could move past my experience and have a healthy relationship. While in counselling, I was advised to write a letter to the molester, so I did; however, in his response, there was no remorse.

It was not a subject that was easy to share. Being a quiet child, I kept it to myself for years. I did not know how to communicate such shame and despair to anyone. It took a long time to feel comfortable talking about this ordeal or even feel comfortable in my own skin. These were the times I had to lean on God to find stability within myself and trust that it would dawn a brighter day.

> Hear my cry O God; attend unto my prayer. From the end of the earth will I cry unto thee, when my heart is overwhelmed lead me to the rock that is higher than I. (Psalms 61:1–2)

For many years, I felt an inability to communicate my feelings about my past. It was an unwelcomed cloud hanging over me. At times, I tried to rid myself of the memory, but it took time to diminish in my mind.

God was my source of strength because no matter what time of day it was, I could always turn to him in prayer to heal my brokenness and lift my burdens. A song I remember says, "Jesus took my burdens I could no longer bear; Jesus took my burden he answered to my prayer; my anxious fears subsided my spirit was made strong, for Jesus took my burden and left me with a song."

11

A Blessing Out of a Curse

My children are a blessing. The older daughter was quiet, yet independent. As a matter of fact, both of my children are independent. My older child is in the United States Navy and is focused on her objectives. My younger daughter is an extrovert like her dad; she is friendly and loves people.

My children have brought a lot of joy to my life. My husband is also a blessing, a man who is easy to talk to and has experience in counselling, a man who is caring and has the ability to put aside his feelings and deal with the issue at hand. He helped me to better communicate my feelings. I also learned to trust individuals more than I had before. I was also able to build more friendships.

My husband is very understanding and patient. I was able to share with him and lean on him when needed for support. This newfound love gave me the strength to close the old chapter of my life and begin a new chapter with the man I love. This new chapter brought happiness. I was able to move on with my life, feeling more settled within myself and liberated from my past.

The blessing came at a good time in my life because I was able to have more children and share in marriage with my husband. It had always been my desire to marry and have more children.

Marriage came at the age of thirty-eight. Maybe it took that long to sort through my past and become whole again. My being a mother again was not as difficult because my husband and I worked together.

The second child is more of an extrovert like her father. Praise God we are a close-knit family. I trust that God will continue to bless us as a family that we continue to grow and flourish. My husband has brought much comfort and stability to me over the years. He is a strong and a no-nonsense person; I feel safe and comfortable in the relationship and blessed as we share our lives together. I'm able to share and discuss my past with my husband whose background in counselling has been an added benefit. We continue to grow together as a couple in the fear of God and trust God will bless our endeavors. As the saying goes, trouble doesn't last always.

The steps of a good man are ordered by the Lord:
and he delighteth in his way. (Psalms 37:23)

12
Too Risky

Thinking back over this ordeal, I'm reminded that I'm so blessed. You see, I found out later on that the perpetrator had a background. He used to sleep with prostitutes, so I thought to myself if God had not kept him safe, it may have been my demise. If this person had contracted HIV, I could have been infected, and it would be detrimental.

I cannot begin to imagine what I would have done if my life would have taken a different turn. I am here for a purpose. What the devil meant for evil, God turned it around for good. My older daughter could have been infected. I shudder to think if God had not kept us what life would be like.

There's a song that says, "I'm here today because God kept me, I'm alive today because of his grace he kept me, God's mercy kept me, so I wouldn't let go."

What a blessing to know I'm kept by the Lord! I believe I need to embrace life more and take more time to smell the roses.

There's a chorus that says, "He hideth my soul in the cleft of the rock that shadows a dry thirsty land, He hideth my life in the depth of his love, And covers me there with his hand, And covers me there with his hand."

God has kept me through the good times and bad times. I owe him my life.

> If it had not been the Lord who was on our side, now may Israel say; If it had not been the Lord who was on our side, when men rose up against

us: Then they had swallowed us up quick, when their wrath was kindled against us: Then the waters had overwhelmed us, the stream had gone over our soul. (Psalms 124:1–4)

Because God was on my side, I am here today, giving thanks.

13

FORGIVENESS

Forgiving for me was challenging at times. I used to question God as to why he allowed molestation at a young age and later why I was a victim of rape. It really gripped me for a long time the reason for such pain. I trust God who knows all things and is able to keep that which I have committed unto him against that day. Maybe through my experience, I can help someone to get past their experience. I'm still able to sing the song "He Never Failed Me Yet."

It has been such a life of struggle, even though I was born in the church. This plagued my mind for many years. I was brought up in church and experienced so many downfalls and negativity, and people who I expected better from tried preventing me from moving forward because they felt I was not good enough.

At times, I wonder why my perpetrators succumb to what they did. Maybe they were hurt as children themselves and became victimizers. I hope they find God in their lives and heal and become better people. I wish them the best and hope they live healthy productive lives.

After much soul-searching over the years, I have learned to let it go. It was a process. Eventually, I was able to forgive the perpetrators and move forward. At times, I would pray and leave it and then pick it up at a later date. I believe it took divine healing to completely be released from my past.

Now I'm free and no longer bound. It's a blessing to forgive, because it leaves a peace and cultivated joy. There's freedom to move beyond what happened and focus on the present and future.

14
DELIVERANCE

Even through life's challenges and heartrending experiences, I have learned to lean on God in prayer and trust his Word. Isaiah 55:9–12 is a promise that has been encouraging:

> For as the heavens are higher than the earth, so are my ways higher than your ways and my thoughts than your thoughts. For as the rain cometh down, and the snow from heaven, and returneth not thither, but watereth the earth, and maketh it bring forth and bud, that it may give seed to the sower, and bread to the eater: so shall my word be that goeth forth out of my mouth: it shall not return unto me void, but it shall accomplish that which I please, and it shall prosper in the thing whereto I sent it. For ye shall go out with joy, and be led forth with peace: the mountains and the hills shall break forth before you into singing, and all the trees of the field shall clap their hands.

This word encourages that whatsoever the Lord promises, it shall not return without accomplishment. God's Word cannot return to him void. It has to achieve that which it is sent to do.

My help cometh from the Lord… (Psalms 121:2)

I'm encouraged in believing the worst is behind me and that better lies ahead. There is a peace in my life now after years of turmoil and anguish, but thanks be to God, I am settled and moving forth in victory. I'm a new person today. Being married to an extrovert who loves people, I had to relearn how to communicate with others, and to some extent, how to trust again. Trusting again brought a balance in the relationship and was good for my overall health. Thanks be to God! I can say I've come a long way. My greatest help and strength come from the Lord, abiding in his Word and using it daily as my guide.

Trouble doesn't last always. We are overcomers through Christ Jesus.

> But without faith it is impossible to please him: for he that cometh to God must believe that he is, and that he is a rewarder of them that diligently seek him. (Hebrews 11:6)

I've written this book as a testimony and closure to my personal struggles. I've held my children close and encouraged them to be aware of unwelcome gestures that they may encounter from strangers or family members. My hope is that in reading this book, if you have experienced molestation, rape, or depression, know there is a God who is able to help you overcome. I would say more, but I want to protect my daughters.

I not only have a testimony. I am a testimony. I know troubles will not last always. It has dawned a better day.

It was not easy to write this book. I often cried as I poured my soul into sharing my personal and painful story in hopes that it would help anyone who has ever suffered pain, abuse, trauma, or sorrow that has left you broken. But it was worth it. I cried because I realized that I had been delivered. Even though this book exposes the most traumatic experiences of my life, it also testifies to the unmeasurable love and grace of God. That was what helped me to overcome.

I realize that my ability to open up and share my story without reservation to a world that can be so critical and cold is a testament to my healing. The innocent little girl who was molested approximately forty-seven years ago has grown into a self-confident and self-assured woman who is no longer bound by the shame of her past. As an emotionally damaged young woman who was already struggling with the legacy of child sexual abuse, then brutally raped twice in my twenties, I stepped forward to share my story in confidence.

But this story is not just about me. This story belongs to many other victims and survivors who are still impeded by the scars of their experiences. I wrote this book for us all and as a means to finally break free from what had held me tied up for so long. If I can be free, so can you.

Whatever your story maybe, I want you to know that I can relate. I too struggled with low self-esteem and mental health issues that are usually the fruit that survivors of molestation and rape are left to endure. But I made it, and so can you.

My prayer is that we all will be overcomers and that by reading this book, we will be encouraged and convinced that we do not have to remain in the misery of their stories.

Here are some of the key messages that I would have shared with my younger self had I thought about them or had the strength to consider them. I believe this guidance would have helped me along my journey:

I encourage you make yourself and your recovery a priority. No matter how long you have carried this burden, whether it is a pain that you experienced fifty years ago or yesterday, I want to encourage you to embark upon an intentional plan to overcome your situation so that your circumstances do not control and/or ruin your life.

Believe in yourself. Although this circumstance happened to you, it is not the end of your life. I do not say this to trivialize your experience. What I want to do is to encourage you to move forward by believing that you are special, you have a purpose, and that you matter. What happened to you is not your fault. Your experience is only one part of your story, and you and only you can control the narrative. I encourage you not to give the perpetrator power over you. There is nothing wrong with you.

Do not suffer in silence. From my experience, keeping your pain, the traumatic event that you have endured, and suffering alone will do more damage than good. You do not have anything to be embarrassed about. The recent "Me Too" movement is proof that although slow, increasingly, society is rejecting those that violate women and those who are vulnerable. There are many therapists and social workers, doctors, and counsellors that you can reach out to. If you are in an area or situation where you cannot physically meet with anyone, there are teleconferences and other online resources that will enable you to access the help you need.

There are resources in your community that you can access. Call a local church, speak to your doctor, find someone who you can speak to that can support you and help you to shoulder the burden. I believe that if I had confided in someone when I was struggling, I would not have attempted to take my life.

Hold on to the belief that things can and will get better. Use faith to guide you through the process of healing. Faith in God will help you along the way. Faith in God and not in a religion, doctrine, creed, or club is what will help you through.

My faith in God is the anthem of this book. By the grace of God, I made it. He is the reason for my testimony. He is the reason for my deliverance. God has been the constant in my life. He has had that little girl in the palm of his hand, and he kept me when I was alone. He was there. He never left me nor forsook me. Throughout this painful journey, my faith brought me through. I proved God for myself. I proved that God is real and that he loves me, and I was able to stand upon his truths about me and his love for me through his son, Jesus Christ.

Over and over, God brought me through even the days when I regressed and focused on my pain rather than my faith. Even when I tried to end my life, he was there.

Maybe you are reading this book and have never prayed, have never thought about praying, and have never read the Bible. Or maybe your experiences have caused you to lose your faith. Whatever faith or beliefs you may or may not have, it's never too late to pray. Through prayer, I promise you will become an overcomer just like me. Your prayer does not have to be full of grand words. A simple request for help and acknowledgment of God is where you can start. God is not concerned with how fancy or how long your prayer is. He wants to access your heart so he can heal it. So if you want to pray and don't know how, you can start here:

> Dear God, this is XXX.
>
> I am hurting and need help. I ask that you reveal yourself to me. I have never prayed before, but nothing else has worked for me, so I am now going to try asking you to help me. Help me and show me how to overcome the tragic experiences that I have endured. Please prove yourself to me...

Take one step at a time and pray this prayer, believing that God will answer you.

You will find that God will speak back to you and respond to you through his Word. You will be amazed at how he will speak to you and will help you move forward to greater strength and peace. By making a point to read the Bible, the Word of God, you will immediately become acquainted with the wonderful promises and plans that he has for you.

In the Bible are the promises of help, love, peace, and prosperity that God has made to his children. Though you may be broken and hurting, you are his child, and he cares for you.

I encourage you to read some of these promises and begin to remind him of the promises that he made in his Word. If you need peace, ask him for peace. If you need to feel his love, ask him to love on you. If you need to forgive, ask him to show you how and to help you to forgive.

The following scriptures are just a handful of some of the promises from a father to his children that I have embraced and that you too can use to strengthen you in your journey.

> For God so loved the world, that he gave his only begotten Son, that whosoever believeth in him should not perish, but have everlasting life. (John 3:16)

Psalms 147:3 promises that, "He heals the brokenhearted, and bind up their wounds." In Isaiah 41:10, he reminds that we should remember that he will help us: "So do not fear; for I am with you; do not be dismayed, for I am your God. I will strengthen you; I will help you; I will uphold you with my righteous hand."

> For I know the plans I have for you, declares the Lord, plans to prosper you and not to harm you, plans to give you hope and a future. (Jeremiah 29:11)

> Come to me, all you who are weary and burdened, and I will give you rest. (Matthew 11:28)

> God is our refuge and strength, an ever-present help in trouble. Therefore, we will not fear, though the earth gives way and the mountains fall into the heart of the sea. (Psalm 46:1–2)

Above all remember, you can make it. Trouble doesn't last always. Find a Bible-based church and make God the Lord of your life.